Tsunamis

By Megan Kopp

AV² provides enriched content that supplements and complements this book. Weigl's AV² books strive to create inspired learning and engage young minds in a total learning experience.

Your AV² Media Enhanced books come alive with...

Audio
Listen to sections of the book read aloud.

Key Words
Study vocabulary, and complete a matching word activity.

Video
Watch informative video clips.

Quizzes
Test your knowledge.

Embedded Weblinks
Gain additional information for research.

Slide Show
View images and captions, and prepare a presentation.

Try This!
Complete activities and hands-on experiments.

... and much, much more!

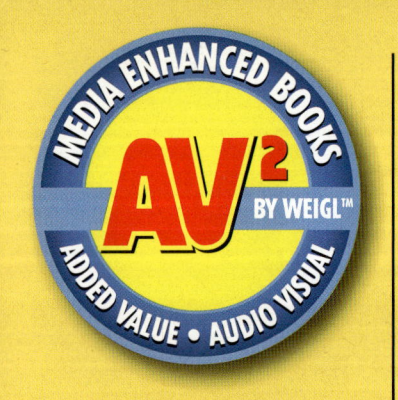

Go to www.av2books.com, and enter this book's unique code.

BOOK CODE

B980668

AV² by Weigl brings you media enhanced books that support active learning.

Published by AV² by Weigl
350 5th Avenue, 59th Floor
New York, NY 10118
Websites: www.av2books.com   www.weigl.com

Copyright ©2015 AV² by Weigl
All rights reserved. No part of this publication may be reproduced, stored in a retrieval system, or transmitted in any form or by any means, electronic, mechanical, photocopying, recording, or otherwise, without the prior written permission of the publisher.

Library of Congress Control Number: 2014934889
ISBN 978-1-4896-1218-2 (hardcover)
ISBN 978-1-4896-1219-9 (softcover)
ISBN 978-1-4896-1220-5 (single-user eBook)
ISBN 978-1-4896-1221-2 (multi-user eBook)

Printed in the United States of America in North Mankato, Minnesota
1 2 3 4 5 6 7 8 9 0 18 17 16 15 14

052014
WEP090514

Senior Editor: Aaron Carr
Art Director: Terry Paulhus

Every reasonable effort has been made to trace ownership and to obtain permission to reprint copyright material. The publishers would be pleased to have any errors or omissions brought to their attention so that they may be corrected in subsequent printings.

Photo Credits
Weigl acknowledges Getty Images as its primary photo supplier for this title.

Contents

AV² Book Code 2

Tsunamis are One of the Deadliest Natural Disasters
   in the World 4

Most Tsunamis are Caused by Earthquakes 6

Tsunamis Cannot be Prevented 8

Tsunamis Happen Around the World
   More Often Than You Think 10

All-Time Records 12

Tsunamis in the United States 14

Japan Experiences the Most Tsunamis
   of Any Country in the World 16

The DART Tsunami Warning System
   Helps Provide Early Warning 18

Little Known Facts 20

A Tsunami is Mostly Deadly When the Largest
   Waves Reach the Shore 22

Tsunamis Damage Large Structures 24

Myths 26

Tsunami Timeline 28

Test Your knowledge 29

Create a Disaster Kit 30

Key Words/Index 31

Log on to www.av2books.com 32

Tsunamis are One of the Deadliest Natural Disasters in the World

Tsunamis are large waves caused by a sudden movement of the ocean floor. These large waves are most common in areas around the Pacific Ocean. This includes Japan, Chile, and the west coast of the United States. In the middle of the ocean, the waves are small. As they approach land, they slow down and grow in height. These waves can travel across the ocean at speeds up to 500 miles (800 kilometers) per hour. By the time a tsunami wave reaches the shore, it may be as high as 100 feet (30 meters). These fast-moving walls of water cause a great deal of damage when they crash into cities and towns along the coast.

The word tsunami is Japanese. *Tsu* means "harbor," and *Nami* means "wave."

Tsunamis were once called tidal waves. This is misleading because these waves have nothing to do tides.

Most Tsunamis are Caused by Earthquakes

Most tsunamis are caused by earthquakes. Tsunamis can also be caused by landslides, volcanic eruptions, and **meteor** impacts. Any large force that causes a sudden and major shift in the ocean floor can create a tsunami.

CAUSES OF TSUNAMIS

Earthquakes

Not all earthquakes create tsunamis. In order to cause a tsunami, an earthquake must be under or near the ocean. It must also be strong enough to move the ocean floor up or down many feet (meters) over a large area. This area may be up to 38,600 square miles (100,000 square kilometers).

Landslides

Underwater landslides are often caused by earthquakes. Tsunamis created by above water forces usually disappear quickly and do not affect distant coastlines. In 1958, a landslide in Lituya Bay, Alaska, created a massive tsunami. The wave reached higher on land than any other tsunami in history.

Volcanic Eruptions

Volcanoes can cause tsunamis in two ways. One can happen when a volcano on land breaks apart and forces large amounts of **debris** into water. This sudden change displaces the water and causes waves. Tsunamis can also be created by underwater volcanoes that collapse or explode.

Meteor Impacts

Like landslides, this force disturbs the water from the top. Resulting tsunamis are usually short-lived. They do not reach as far as earthquake tsunamis. They are also not very common.

NATURAL DISASTERS

Tsunami waves are not like waves created by wind. Waves that come crashing into a beach after a storm in the Pacific Ocean are rhythmic. They follow a set pattern. Each wave is a set time away from the following wave. This time may vary, but it is usually about 10 seconds. Each wave is less than 500 feet (150 m) long. Tsunami waves can be up to one hour apart and more than 60 miles (100 km) long. These deadly waves also spread quickly and travel great distances without losing much of their strength.

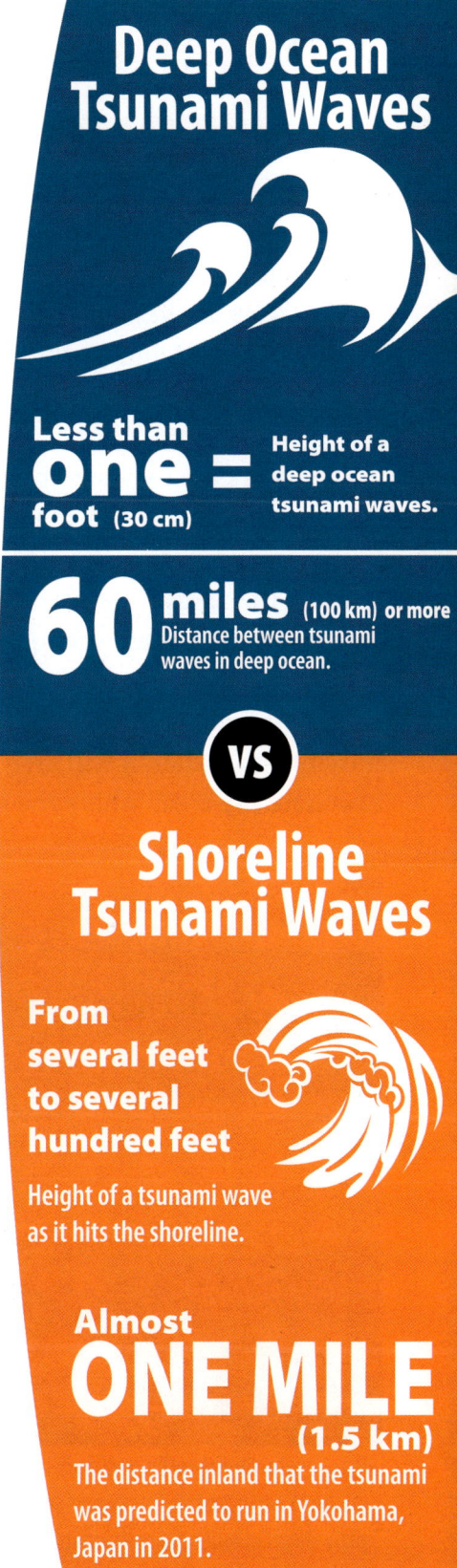

In 2004, a massive earthquake in the Indian Ocean caused one of the most destructive tsunamis ever recorded. Tsunami waves caused widespread damage and deaths to 11 nearby countries.

Deep Ocean Tsunami Waves

Less than one foot (30 cm) = Height of a deep ocean tsunami waves.

60 miles (100 km) or more Distance between tsunami waves in deep ocean.

VS

Shoreline Tsunami Waves

From several feet to several hundred feet Height of a tsunami wave as it hits the shoreline.

Almost ONE MILE (1.5 km) The distance inland that the tsunami was predicted to run in Yokohama, Japan in 2011.

TSUNAMIS 7

Tsunamis Cannot be Prevented

Tsunamis cannot be predicted or prevented. Scientists are working to better understand how natural events such as tsunamis and earthquakes work. They hope to one day be able to predict when and where these events will take place.

Today, there are two tsunami warning centers in the United States. They are located in Hawai'i and Alaska. These warning centers, along with others around the world, try to warn people when a tsunami is coming their way. These centers gather information from around the world. As soon as an earthquake or volcano eruption is detected, the information is sent to the warning centers. Scientists at the centers then figure out which direction the tsunami is traveling, how fast it is moving, and when it will arrive on shore. They then warn people to **evacuate** the areas where the tsunami will hit.

People who live near the ocean must be aware of earthquakes. It is important to plan ahead in order to know what to do in the event of a tsunami.

When a tsunami hit Hilo, Hawai'i, in 1946, there was no warning of its arrival. After that, a tsunami warning system was created. Scientists kept a close watch on earthquake activity and the measurement of tsunami waves at **tide gauges** in harbors. Tsunami warnings were issued if it looked like there was danger. Unfortunately, this was not very accurate.

Since 1946, 20 tsunami warnings have been given. Only five of these tsunamis were strong enough to cause damage, and 15 were false alarms. In Alaska, scientists have recently developed a series of deep ocean tsunami detectors. They provide the accurate information needed to predict tsunamis.

Some coastal cities and towns use public address systems with loud speakers to warn people of approaching tsunamis.

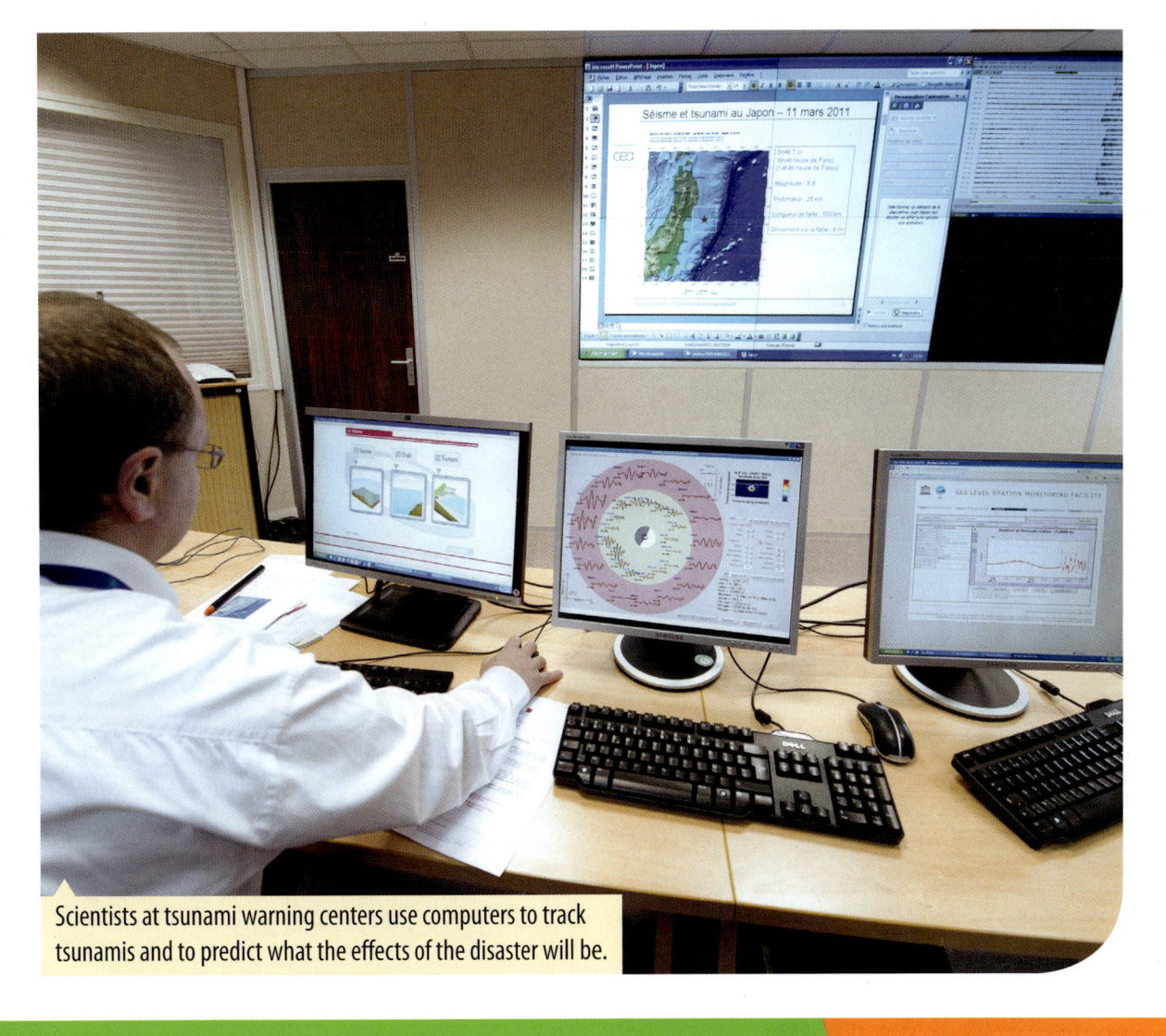

Scientists at tsunami warning centers use computers to track tsunamis and to predict what the effects of the disaster will be.

TSUNAMIS 9

Tsunamis Happen Around the World More Often Than You Think

Scientists can study **sediments** left by large tsunamis in the past. This helps them better understand tsunamis. In the Pacific Ocean, there have been almost 1,500 tsunamis dating back to 47 BC. In the past 100 years, there have been about 650 tsunamis. This is an average of six or seven tsunamis each year. Not all of these tsunamis caused much damage, however.

Tsunamis have been recorded in all oceans of the world. Most take place in the Pacific Ring of Fire. This is a string of 452 underwater volcanoes in the shape of a 25,000-mile (40,000-km) long horseshoe. The Ring of Fire is what causes more earthquakes and tsunamis to happen in the Pacific Ocean than anywhere else on Earth.

The Indian and Atlantic Oceans are less geologically active than the Pacific, so tsunamis happen there less often.

Japan has had more than 200 tsunamis in the past 1,300 years. In 1498, 31,000 people died in a tsunami in Japan. In 1755, a massive earthquake in Lisbon, Portugal created a tsunami that was felt in Portugal, Spain, Morocco, and the United Kingdom. Waves traveled as far away as Barbados. More recently, on September 29, 2009, a shallow earthquake with a **magnitude** of 8.3 caused a tsunami in Samoa. In 2010, an earthquake near Haiti caused a tsunami that left more than 220,000 people dead.

The 2004 Indian Ocean tsunami was caused by a magnitude 9 earthquake near the coast of Indonesia and Sumatra.

About 86%
of all tsunamis are caused by underwater earthquakes, or "seaquakes."

36,000
The number of people killed when the volcano **Krakatoa** erupted in the East Indies on **August 27, 1883**. It created a 100-foot (30-m) high tsunami.

More than 420,000
The number of lives lost to tsunamis since 1850.

Over 1/2 a Million
Houses and buildings destroyed during 2011 tsunami and earthquake in Japan.

TSUNAMIS

All-Time Records

The first tsunami recorded by people who watched it happen took place in Switzerland in 1601. Every since, people have been studying tsunamis to try to understand what causes them and how people can be better prepared for them.

DEADLIEST
The deadliest tsunami ever took place on December 26, 2004, in the Indian Ocean. The tsunami led to the deaths of 830,000 people.

BIGGEST
The highest magnitude of tsunami in the last 100 years was in Chile in 1960. It had the most energy released during its formation and moved the largest amount of water.

HIGHEST
The tsunami wave with the highest runup, or splash, was in Lituya Bay, Alaska, in 1958. The water ran more than 1,700 feet (525 m) up the hillsides.

Worst Tsunami Caused by a Landslide
On October 9, 1963, rocks tumbled into the Vaiont Reservoir in Italy. The force of the landslide created a tsunami that caused 3,000 deaths.

Tsunamis in the United States

Runup is a term used to describe the **vertical** wave height of a tsunami at a given point above sea level. Counting only tsunamis with a runup of more than 3 feet (1 m), there have been more than 30 tsunamis since 1811 in Hawai'i. Alaska has had 16 tsunamis since 1853. There have been close to another 30 tsunamis along the U.S. west coast since 1912. Puerto Rico, the U.S. Virgin Islands, and Guam also have history of tsunamis.

RISK OF TSUNAMI
- EXTREME RISK
- HIGH RISK
- MEDIUM RISK
- LOW RISK
- VERY LOW RISK

MAP SCALE
0 — 500 miles / 500 kilometers

14 NATURAL DISASTERS

ALASKA

Alaska

Pacific Ocean

HAWAI'I

Kaua`i
Ni`ihau
Oahu
Moloka`i
Maui
Hawai'i

Pacific Ocean

North Dakota
Minnesota
South Dakota
Lake Superior
Wisconsin
Lake Huron
Lake Michigan
Michigan
Lake Ontario
New York
Lake Erie
Pennsylvania
Nebraska
Iowa
Illinois
Indiana
Ohio
West Virginia
Virginia
Kansas
Missouri
Kentucky
Oklahoma
Arkansas
Tennessee
North Carolina
South Carolina
Mississippi
Alabama
Georgia
Texas
Louisiana
Florida

New Hampshire
Vermont
Maine
Massachusetts
Rhode Island
Connecticut
New Jersey
Delaware
Maryland

Atlantic Ocean

Gulf of Mexico

TSUNAMIS 15

Japan Experiences the Most Tsunamis of Any Country in the World

Of all the countries in the world, Japan is the one most often hit by tsunamis. Japan is located where four pieces of the Earth's **crust** meet. The movement of these pieces of crust, called tectonic plates, causes thousands of earthquakes every year.

Tsunami waves have enough force to throw huge ships onto shore.

16 NATURAL DISASTERS

Tsunami science and engineering began in Japan. In 1896, a tsunami claimed thousands of lives. A tide record was used for the first time to prove that this tsunami was created by an earthquake. In 1933, the same area was hit again by another large tsunami. A series of measures to protect against tsunami damage was put forward. Houses were moved, and the first tsunami breakwater structures were built. In 1941, tsunami **forecasting** began. Since the late 1970s, tsunami **modeling** using information from a variety of sources was developed in Japan. This modeling format is now used in 22 countries around the world.

Even with all of the work scientists around the world have done to provide early warnings, some tsunamis strike too quickly. People do not have time to evacuate in these tsunamis.

6,834
Pounds (3,100 kg) of weight used to anchor floating sensors used to study tsunamis.

Less than 20 miles (30 km)
The depth underground that a tsunami earthquake is found.

1998 On July 17 of this year, a magnitude 7 earthquake caused an underwater landslide.

Three waves measuring more than 23 feet (7 m) hit a 6-mile (10-km) stretch of Papua New Guinea coastline within 10 minutes.

3 INCHES (8 cm)
The distance that the tectonic plates move near Japan each year.

TSUNAMIS 17

The DART Tsunami Warning System Helps Provide Early Warning

Tsunamis are detected by special open ocean **buoys** and coastal tide gauges. In the United States, these instruments send their data to tsunami warning centers in Hawai'i and Alaska. DART stands for Deep-Ocean Assessment and Reporting of Tsunamis. In 2008, Christian Meinig and Scott Stalin received an award for inventing the DART tsunami technology. Christian Meinig is the current Director of Engineering at the National Oceanic & Atmosphere Administration (NOAA). He leads teams of engineers and technicians specializing in ocean and atmospheric study. Scott Stalin is the current Deputy Director of Engineering at NOAA. Until early in 2007, he was the electronics engineer responsible for the computing and electronic systems for DART.

It takes a crew of several people and the help of a crane to place a DART buoy in the ocean.

The NOAA first placed the DART system in six locations in 2001. They were placed in areas with a history of tsunamis. Each DART station is made up of a pressure recorder on the ocean floor and an anchored buoy on the surface. A sound link sends the information recorded on the ocean floor to the buoy on the surface. The surface buoy then sends the information to a satellite. From there, it is sent to tsunami warning centers. The DART system gathers information every 15 minutes. When there is an earthquake or volcanic activity, the system works more quickly. For the first few minutes, it reports every 15 seconds. After that, it sends information once every minute. It will keep doing this for four hours. If there is no more activity, the system switches back to its regular 15-minute cycle.

In 2005, The NOAA announced a plan to improve its tsunami warning system by adding 32 additional DART buoys.

People can visit places such as the Museum of Science in Chicago to see a DART buoy in person.

TSUNAMIS 19

Little Known Facts

KNOW THE WORDS

In Hawai'i there are two words used to describe tsunamis. "Kai e 'e" is used for tsunami waves. "Kai mimiki" refers to the pulling out of the water from the shore before the waves hit.

METEOR SHOWER

Two million years ago a massive meteor hit offshore of Chile. It was about 2.5 miles (4 km) wide. It caused a massive tsunami that swept across parts of South America and Antarctica. Proof of this disaster was discovered by scientists in 1997.

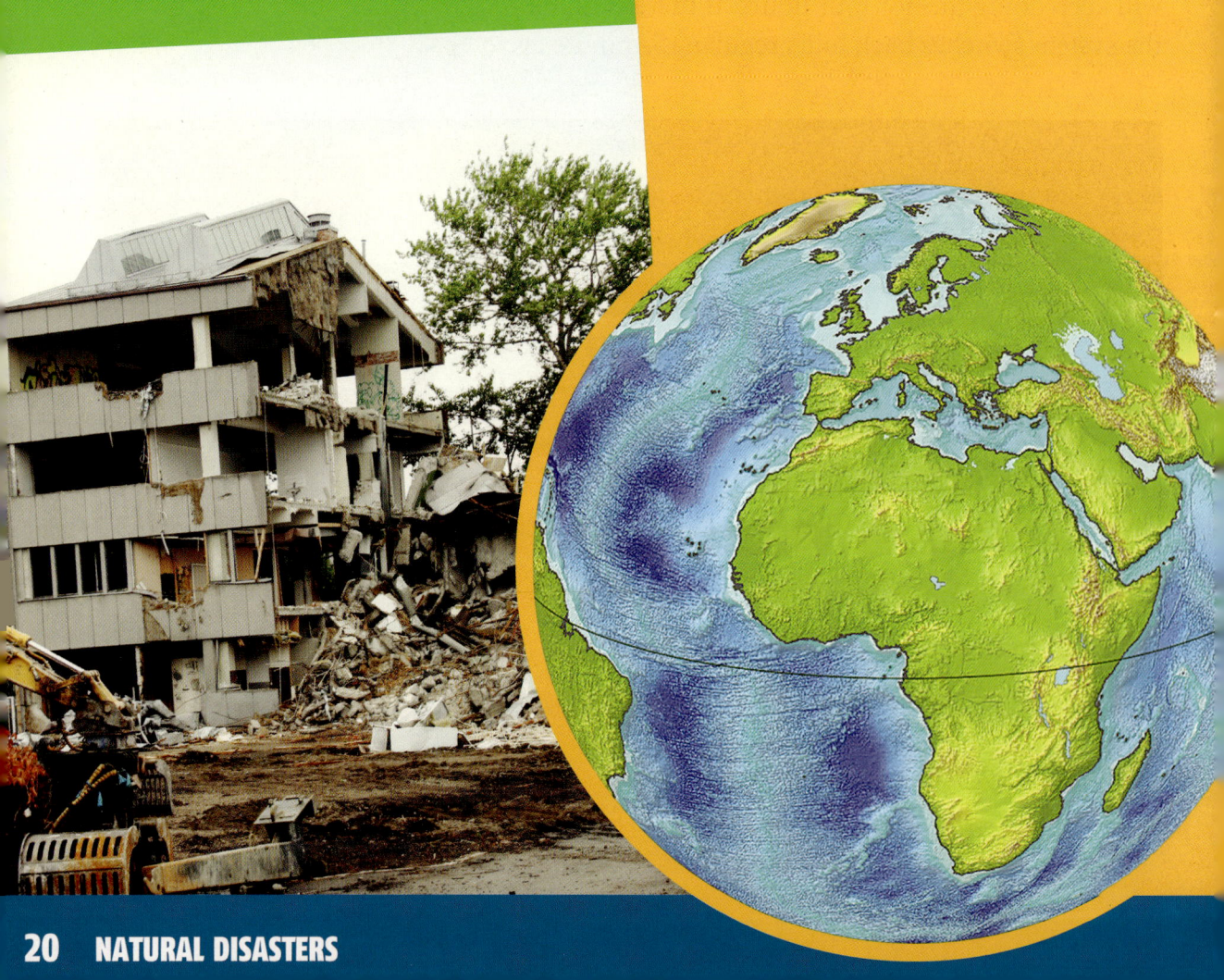

TONS OF ENERGY

The energy released from a magnitude 7 earthquake is about the same as the amount released by a half a megaton nuclear bomb. Still, this is not enough to create a tsunami. A magnitude 9 earthquake is 1,000 times more powerful than a 7. Depending on its location, an earthquake of this magnitude will cause a tsunami.

WASHED AWAY

A magnitude 7 earthquake will not cause a tsunami itself. However, it could cause an underwater landslide. The results can be terrible. On July 17, 1998, an earthquake triggered such an event. Three waves measuring more than 23 feet (7 m) hit a 6-mile (10-km) stretch of Papua New Guinea. In a short 10 minutes, three villages were washed away. More than 2,000 people died.

BIGGEST WAVE

In 1737, a huge tsunami hit Cape Lopatka in Kamchatka, Russia. The wave was estimated to be 210 feet (64 m) high.

TSUNAMIS 21

A Tsunami is Most Deadly When the Largest Waves Reach the Shore

The first sign of a tsunami is often the sudden pulling back of the ocean. In a large tsunami, fish can be left flopping on bare sea floor and boats tied up near shore are left sitting on the ground. This is a trough, or low point between the high points of two waves. A tsunami is not a single wave. It is a series of waves called a wave train. The first wave arrives a few minutes later. The remaining waves follow anywhere from 10 minutes to one hour after the first wave. It is important to know that the first wave in a tsunami is not the largest or the most dangerous.

Many coastal towns put up break walls along the waterfront. These walls are meant to stop waves and rising water, but they cannot hold back large tsunami waves.

Tsunami waves move in unexpected directions and have a great deal of power. These waves can move large boulders, destroy homes, and flip vehicles. Debris is tossed around, creating even more of a hazard for anyone caught in its path.

There is no stopping a tsunami. Getting people out the way quickly is important. Tsunamis created close to shore can strike within minutes. In Hawai'i, signs show the path for getting to higher ground quickly. Sirens mounted on tall metal poles sound during a tsunami warning. A tsunami created in Japan will take seven to eight hours to reach Hawai'i. A tsunami from Chile could take more than 14 hours to reach the islands.

HOW TSUNAMI WAVES RISE

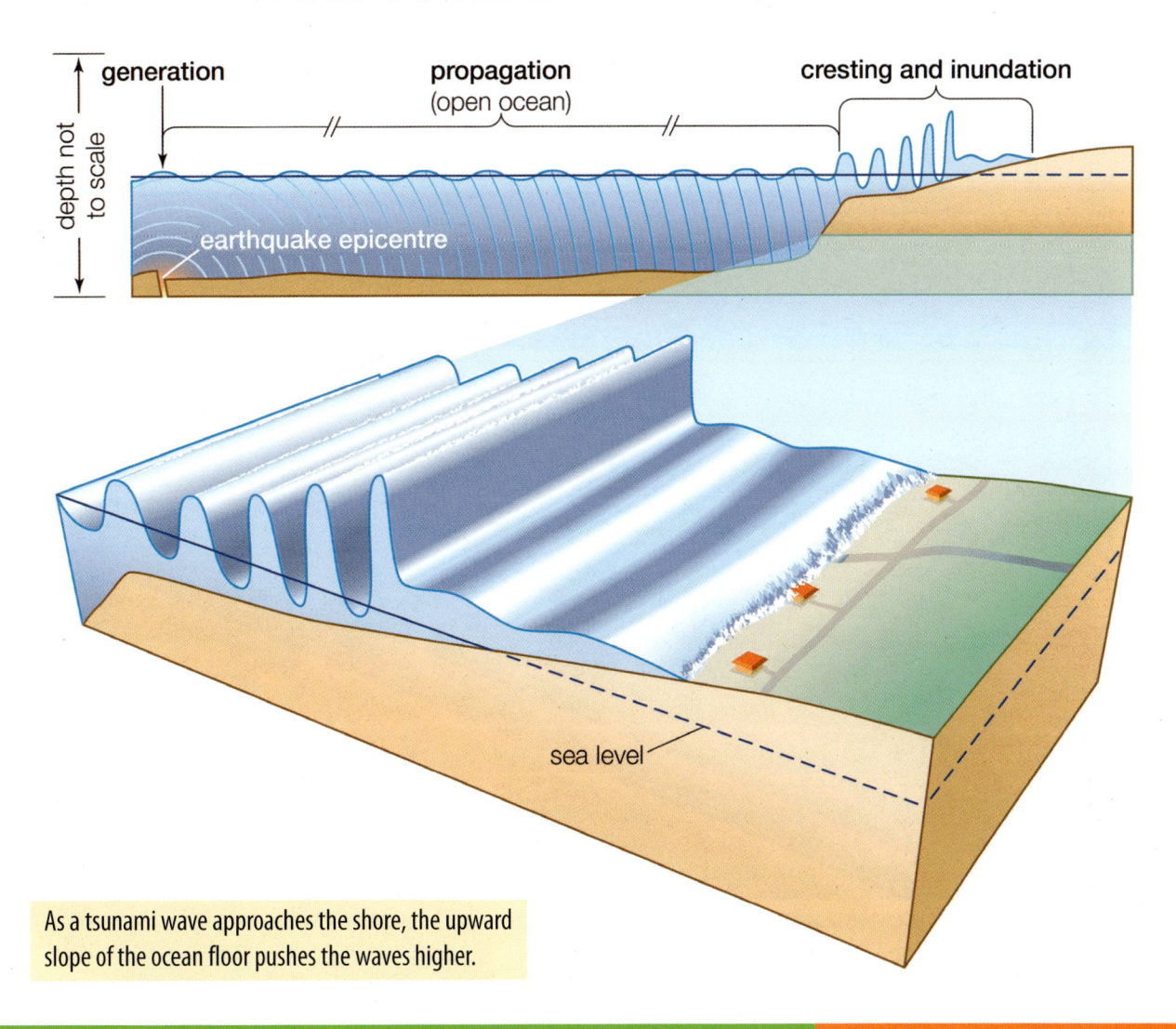

As a tsunami wave approaches the shore, the upward slope of the ocean floor pushes the waves higher.

TSUNAMIS 23

Tsunamis Damage Large Structures

Tsunami damage is not limited to houses and streets. Tsunamis can cause widespread damage to large structures as well. Debris in the waves breaks through walls and crushes roofs. Flooding damages electrical structures. In the 2011 Japan tsunami, salt water entered a nuclear power plant. The plant did not have time to shut down, and it released radioactive material. Buildings such as nuclear power plants will now be built as far away from the coast as possible. They will also be designed to shut down into safe mode as soon as an earthquake happens.

The debris in a tsunami wave may be made up of dirt and rock from the ground, pieces of broken buildings, and even cars and boats.

OTHER TYPES OF DISASTERS

Flooding

Flooding is a major impact of tsunamis. In the Japan tsunami of March 2011, 330 miles (530 km) of coastline was flooded with more than 33 feet (10 m) of seawater. Of that, 124 miles (200 km) had floodwater levels of more than 66 feet (20 m). At its deepest point, the floodwaters from the tsunami were 131 feet (40 m) deep.

Erosion

Scientists working in the Kuril Islands off the east coast of Russia found that tsunamis take away nearly 50 times more sand and soil than they deposit. The amount varies depending on the shape of the land.

Destruction of Ecosystems

The power of the waves in a tsunami is enough to destroy almost anything. Mangrove stands are ripped away, affecting all of the animals that rely on their cover for survival. Fragile coral reefs are stripped bare. Inland soils become **saturated** with salt. They become less productive and many native species of plants are lost.

TSUNAMIS

Myths

There are many stories told around the world that relate to tsunamis. In Sri Lanka, local legends talk about the daughter of a king who was offered to the sea gods. It was hoped that her sacrifice would stop the seas from swallowing villages. In Australia, the Aboriginal legend of the white wave is thought by some to refer to a tsunami that destroyed many villages 200 years ago. The Moken people of the Andamen Islands off the coast of India survived the recent tsunami by paying attention to the warnings of a local shaman, or priest. Changes in the offshore sea life caught their attention and ancient beliefs were carefully followed. When the shaman told everyone to run for higher ground, no one questioned his wisdom. Native American tsunami **myths** also exist along the Pacific Northwest coast in the United States.

The Moken people spend most of the year living at sea in boats carved from a single tree, called a kebang. They only move onto dry land during the rainy monsoon season. During this time, they live in temporary wooden shacks.

The Story Of Thunderbird and the Whale

In the stories from the Pacific Northwest, Thunderbird and Whale are supernatural creatures of great size. Hundreds of years ago, there was a great flood. Thunderbird was fighting with Whale. The fight began in the water, but this was Whale's territory and Thunderbird could not win. He grabbed Whale with his talons and started to fly toward his nest in the mountains. Whale was too large, and Thunderbird dropped him. The waves grew. Thunderbird grabbed Whale again and took off. Before he could reach the mountain, Whale dropped to the ground and the earth shook. Trees were torn away as the pair battled. Again and again, Thunderbird tried to lift Whale. Again he would drop, and the earth would shake. At last Whale escaped back into the sea. Thunderbird gave up the fight and flew to his nest.

Tsunami Timeline

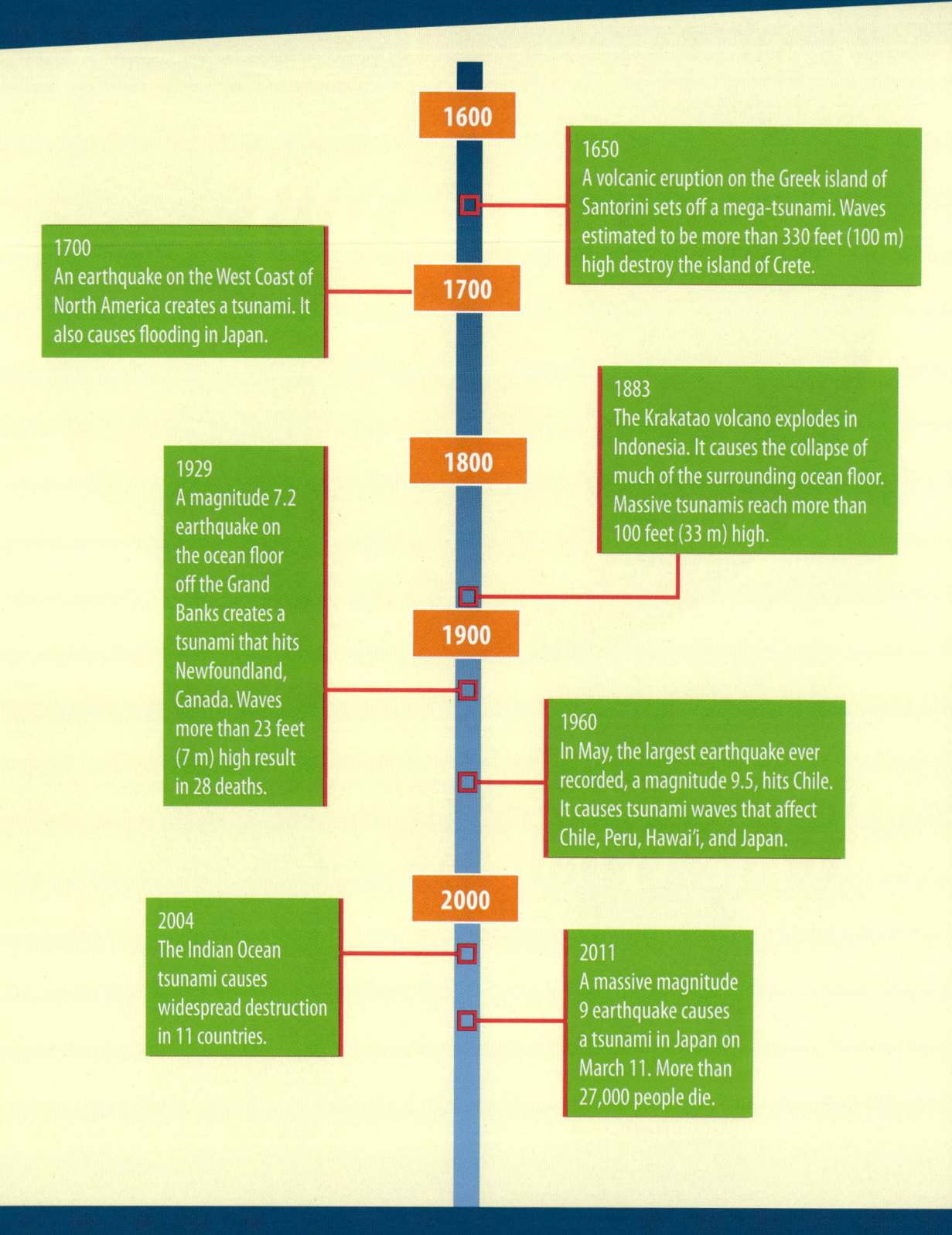

1600

1650
A volcanic eruption on the Greek island of Santorini sets off a mega-tsunami. Waves estimated to be more than 330 feet (100 m) high destroy the island of Crete.

1700
An earthquake on the West Coast of North America creates a tsunami. It also causes flooding in Japan.

1700

1800

1883
The Krakatao volcano explodes in Indonesia. It causes the collapse of much of the surrounding ocean floor. Massive tsunamis reach more than 100 feet (33 m) high.

1929
A magnitude 7.2 earthquake on the ocean floor off the Grand Banks creates a tsunami that hits Newfoundland, Canada. Waves more than 23 feet (7 m) high result in 28 deaths.

1900

1960
In May, the largest earthquake ever recorded, a magnitude 9.5, hits Chile. It causes tsunami waves that affect Chile, Peru, Hawai'i, and Japan.

2000

2004
The Indian Ocean tsunami causes widespread destruction in 11 countries.

2011
A massive magnitude 9 earthquake causes a tsunami in Japan on March 11. More than 27,000 people die.

Test Your Knowledge

1 What is the most common cause of a tsunami?

A. An earthquake

2 Where should people go when a tsunami is approaching?

A. To higher ground

3 On average, how many tsunamis are there each year worldwide?

A. Six or seven

4 How fast can tsunami waves travel?

A. More than 500 miles (800 km) per hour

5 What caused the local tsunami in Lituya Bay, Alaska in 1958?

A. A landslide

6 Will an earthquake measuring 6.0 cause a tsunami?

A. No, earthquakes causing tsunamis measure 7.0 or greater.

7 What does DART stand for?

A. Deep-Ocean Assessment and Reporting of Tsunamis

8 Which country is most often hit by tsunamis?

A. Japan

9 What does the word tsunami mean?

A. In Japanese, *tsu* means "harbor," and *nami* means "wave."

10 Which two scientists received an award for creating the DART system for tsunami reporting?

A. Christian Meinig and Scott Stalin

TSUNAMIS 29

Create a Disaster Kit

Disasters happen anytime and anywhere. Sadly, when an emergency happens, you may not have much time to respond. The Red Cross says that one way to prepare is by assembling an emergency kit. Once disaster hits, you will not have time to shop or search for supplies. If you have gathered supplies in advance, your family will be prepared.

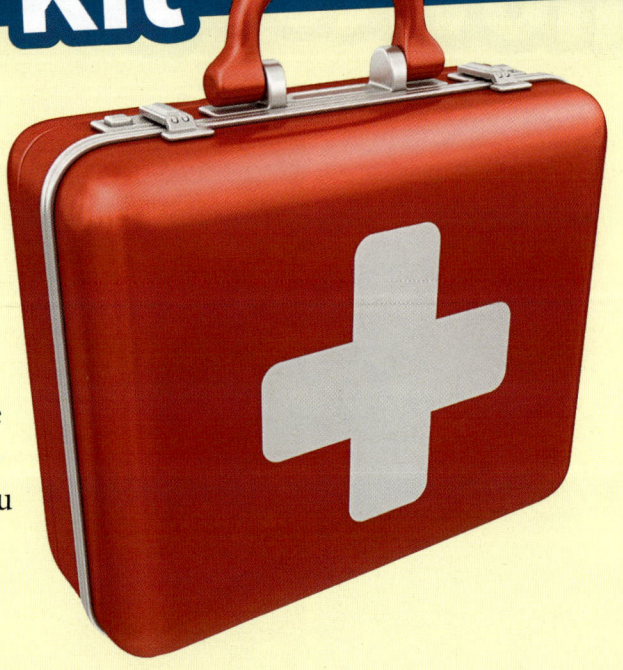

1. Know if your home is in a danger zone. This is based on height above sea level and distance from the coast.

2. Make an evacuation plan. Where will you go? What route will you take to get there? What is an alternate route in case the first route is blocked?

3. Know how to turn off gas, electricity, and water in your home.

4. Know which radio station to listen to for official information about disasters.

5. Build a disaster supply kit.

6. Create an emergency communication plan for getting back together with loved ones if you become separated during a tsunami.

What You Need
- flashlight
- portable, battery-operated radio
- extra batteries
- first aid kit
- emergency food and water
- essential medicines

30 NATURAL DISASTERS

Key Words

buoys: warning floats tied to the ocean floor

crust: the outer rocky layer of the Earth that is made up of many pieces, called tectonic plates, that are always moving

debris: scattered pieces of trash or damaged materials

evacuate: to flee from a place of danger to a safer place

forecasting: to try to predict what will happen in the future

magnitude: the size or importance of something

meteor: a piece of rock or metal from space that speeds into Earth's atmosphere as a streak of light before falling to Earth

modeling: building an example of something larger to see how it will work

myths: stories created by ancient people to explain natural events

saturated: filled with an extremely large amount of something

sediments: materials that settle at the bottom of water

tide gauges: tools for measuring change in sea level

vertical: upright, or going up or down

Index

Alaska 6, 8, 9, 13, 14, 15, 29

Chile 4, 12, 20, 23, 28

DART 18, 19, 29

earthquake 6, 7, 8, 9, 10, 11, 16, 17, 18, 19, 21, 24, 28, 29

Hawai'i 8, 9, 14, 15, 18, 20, 23, 28

Indian Ocean 7, 11, 12, 28

Japan 4, 7, 11, 16, 17, 23, 24, 28, 29

Krakatoa 11, 28

landslide 6, 13, 19, 21, 29

National Oceanic and Atmospheric Administration (NOAA) 18, 19

Pacific Ocean 4, 7, 10, 14, 15, 26, 27

Ring of Fire 10

Russia 21, 25

Sumatra 11

tectonic plates 16, 17

Tsunami Warning System 8, 9, 18, 19, 23

United States 4, 8, 14, 18, 26

volcano 6, 8, 10, 11, 28

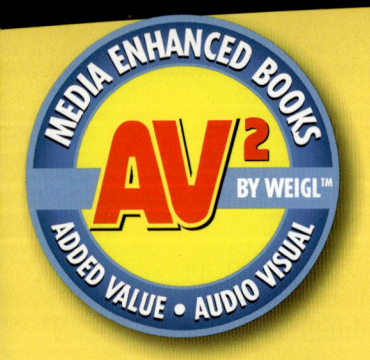

Log on to www.av2books.com

AV² by Weigl brings you media enhanced books that support active learning. Go to www.av2books.com, and enter the special code found on page 2 of this book. You will gain access to enriched and enhanced content that supplements and complements this book. Content includes video, audio, weblinks, quizzes, a slide show, and activities.

AV² Online Navigation

Book Pages
AV² pages directly correspond to pages in the book.

Key Words
Study vocabulary, and complete a matching word activity.

Quizzes
Test your knowledge.

Slide Show
View images and captions, and prepare a presentation.

Audio
Listen to sections of the book read aloud.

Video
Watch informative video clips.

Embedded Weblinks
Gain additional information for research.

Try This!
Complete activities and hands-on experiments.

AV² was built to bridge the gap between print and digital. We encourage you to tell us what you like and what you want to see in the future.

Sign up to be an AV² Ambassador at www.av2books.com/ambassador.

Due to the dynamic nature of the Internet, some of the URLs and activities provided as part of AV² by Weigl may have changed or ceased to exist. AV² by Weigl accepts no responsibility for any such changes. All media enhanced books are regularly monitored to update addresses and sites in a timely manner. Contact AV² by Weigl at 1-866-649-3445 or av2books@weigl.com with any questions, comments, or feedback.